In the Tree

Alex G. Webb

OXFORD
UNIVERSITY PRESS

I am an orangutan.

I swing in the tree.

I eat in the tree.

I play in the tree.

I sleep in the tree.

I am an orangutan.
I live in the tree.

Notes for Teachers and Parents

Before Reading:

- Begin a discussion about orangutans. What do children know about orangutans?
- Encourage the children to tell you what is happening on the cover.
- Have them predict what they think the story is about.
- Read the title together. Point to the first letter of each word as it is spoken.

During Reading:

- Encourage the children to look at the pictures and comment on what they see.
- Draw their attention to key ideas that they don't point out.

After Reading:

- Ask the children to pick their favourite page. Have them tell a story about the picture.
- Encourage the children talk about where they live, describing what they do in their favourite rooms.
- Have the children draw a picture of their home and talk about it when they are finished.